The
ALGONQUIN
LITERARY QUIZ
BOOK

Compiled by

LOUIS D. RUBIN, JR.

with the assistance of
Julia Randall and Jerry Leath Mills

illustrated by Peter Sis

ALGONQUIN BOOKS OF CHAPEL HILL 1990

Published by
Algonquin Books of Chapel Hill
Post Office Box 2225
Chapel Hill, North Carolina 27515–2225
a division of
Workman Publishing Company, Inc.
708 Broadway
New York, New York 10003

© 1990 by Louis D. Rubin, Jr. All rights reserved.
Printed in the United States of America.

Library of Congress Cataloging-in-Publication Data

Rubin, Louis Decimus, 1923–
     The Algonquin literary quiz book / compiled by Louis D. Rubin, Jr.;
     with the assistance of Julia Randall and Jerry Leath Mills.
          p.   cm.
     Compiled from previously published Algonquin literary quiz
     excerpts along with some new ones.
     ISBN 0-945575-50-5
     1. English literature — Examinations, questions, etc. 2. American
     literature — Examinations, questions, etc. 3. Questions and answers.
     4. Literary recreations. I. Randall, Julia, 1923–   . II. Mills,
     Jerry Leath. III. Algonquin Books of Chapel Hill (Firm) IV. Title.
PR87.R8 1990
807.6 — dc20   90-35595
                                                                              CIP

First Printing
10   9   8   7   6   5   4   3   2   1

For the première danseuse
Shannon Ravenel

Prefatory Note

This little book is meant for pleasure pure and simple. It was fun to put together, and I hope it will be fun to use.

The quizzes that follow were not prepared by searching around for obscure or tricky questions. They are based on whims, fancies, and odd associations and are not designed to be Important, or Relevant, or any such thing as that. That's where the fun comes in. One thing is allowed to suggest another. For example, start with the fact that Elizabeth Barrett Browning's dog was named Flush. This might bring to mind that Samuel Johnson's cat was named Hodge. A little more free association, and some checking of facts in books to make sure that memory isn't playing tricks, and something along this line might result:

Numerous authors have been lovers of animals and owners of domestic pets. How many of the following literary cats and dogs can you spot (no pun intended)? Match the descriptions with the names.

a. Dr. Johnson's pet cat

b. one of the cats in T. S. Eliot's *Old Possum's Book of Practical Cats*

c. cat in William Butler Yeats's poem, "The Cat and the Moon"

d. Elizabeth Barrett Browning's lapdog

e. the dog that howls when old Jolyon Forsyte dies in John Galsworthy's *The Forsyte Saga*

f. the Citizen's dog that chases Leopold Bloom down the street in James Joyce's *Ulysses*

g. the best hunting dog that Aleck Maury ever owned, in Caroline

Gordon's story, "The Last Day in
the Field"

h. the housecat that Tom Sawyer fed
patent medicine to in Mark Twain's
Adventures of Tom Sawyer

i. the dog that bit people in James
Thurber's *My Life and Hard Times*

1. Peter
2. Minnaloushe
3. Garryowen
4. Flush
5. Muggs
6. Hodge
7. Gyges
8. Balthazar
9. Macavity

The trick is to match the description, designated by a letter, with the name of the pet, designated by a number. Thus the answer to Dr. Johnson's pet cat would be Hodge, and the solution, given in the back of the book, would be listed as **a-6.**

Of what significance, literary or otherwise, is the information about literary canines and felines? None whatsoever. It is merely that the compiler takes pleasure in remembering the names of the pets in question, and presumably the reader will take pleasure in being able to identify them. And that is the sum and substance of the whole business.

The questions that follow are drawn mainly from the literature of England and the United States, with some from Continental literature appearing here and there. The quizzes are short on the younger contemporary authors and books for several reasons. The principal compiler knows a number of writers and didn't want to include some friends and leave others out. Also, it seemed more likely that readers would be familiar with the older, most-anthologized authors and would probably have read their work in high school and college courses. And there is also the fact that the principal compiler has gotten to be an old geezer himself and so naturally thinks in terms of older writers.

The questions range in difficulty from easy to hard. There is no particular progression or hierarchy involved in the order in which they appear. Readers will probably find that the questions for which no matching answers are given are more demanding than the others.

If you can't answer all these questions, don't fret about it. If you had been making up the questions, I wouldn't have been able to answer all yours, either.

On with the show!

The compiler of this book is grateful to his friends Julia Randall and Jerry Leath Mills for contributing some of the quizzes therein and to Marjorie Corbett Hudson, the capable copyeditor of Algonquin Books of Chapel Hill, for an excellent suggestion about presentation.

L. D. R.
Chapel Hill, North Carolina
January 30, 1990

P.S. — Answers to question above: **a-6; b-9; c-2; d-4; e-8; f-3; g-7; h-1; i-5**

The

ALGONQUIN
LITERARYQUIZ
BOOK

Urban
Bards
❧

*P*oets have traditionally extolled the virtues of the simple life of the countryside, yet almost all of them have been urban dwellers. So-called pastoral poetry, having to do with shepherds tending their flocks and the joys of the countryside, has been written not by or for the shepherds and ploughmen themselves, but by sophisticated literary persons who are using the rural scene to make points about what's wrong with the way that other city folk do things. It's simpler and more clear-cut that way. Sometimes, however, poets do consent to write about city life in verse. Can you match the excerpts with the cities being described? Two of the excerpts, by the way, are about the same city. (For the names of the poet and the poem of each excerpt, see the answers at the back of the book.)

· · · · ·

a. This city now doth, like a garment,
   wear
   The beauty of the morning; silent,
   bare,
   Ships, towers, domes, theatres, and
   temples lie
   Open unto the fields, and to the sky

b. Come and show me another city with
   lifted head singing so proud to be
   alive and coarse and strong and
   cunning.
   Flinging magnetic curses amid the
   toil of piling job on job, here is a
   tall bold slugger set vivid against
   the little soft cities

c. Ah, what can ever be more stately
   and admirable to me than mast-
   hemm'd _____ ?
   River and sunset and scallop-edg'd
   waves of flood-tide?
   The sea-gulls oscillating their
   bodies, the hay-boat in the
   twilight,
   and the belated lighter?

d. I wander through each charter'd
   street
   Near where the charter'd _____
   does flow
   And mark in every face I meet
   Marks of weakness, marks of woe

e. In _____, a town of monks and
     bones,
   And pavements fang'd with
     murderous stones
   And rags, and hags, and hideous
     wenches,
   I counted two and seventy stenches

f. I have met them at close of day
   Coming with vivid faces
   From counter or desk among gray
   Eighteenth-century houses

g. The Aquarium is gone now.
     Everywhere,
   giant finned cars nose forward like
     fish;
   A savage servility
   slides by on grease

1. Boston, Massachusetts

2. Chicago, Illinois

3. Cologne, West Germany

4. London, England

5. New York, New York

6. Dublin, Ireland

3

The Strenuous Life

❧

*E*xercise is what Mark Twain said that whenever he got the urge to do it, he took a nap. But the strenuous life has its attractions. In fact, when you get right down to it, Mark Twain lived a pretty active life in his day—piloting a steamboat, prospecting for silver, traveling extensively, going on lengthy lecture tours by rail, playing pool until the wee hours of the morning, and so on. And one thing does seem certain: people enjoy reading about polar expeditions, sea voyages, lengthy journeys, going places in general. The following is a list of outdoor expeditions. Identify the author and the work in which each takes place.

. . . . .

a. a boat trip on New England rivers

b. a trout-fishing expedition near Roncesvalles

c. spelunking on an island in the Mississippi River

d. a tour of the islands of North Scotland

e. a stroll along the banks of the Vivonne

f. a hike from Southwark to an English cathedral

g. a walk from Washington, D.C., to Mount Vernon

Bright
College Years

Youth will have its fling, and frequently on campus. A whaling ship may have been Herman Melville's Yale College or Harvard, and Leopold Bloom and Ernest Hemingway may have done their studying in the University of Life, but more often than not your author of books is an Old Grad who looks back on college years with mixed emotions: he didn't get chosen by the Dekes or elected to ODK, but he did make Phi Beta Kappa and learn to drink beer, etc. Can you match the letters for the following novels with the numbers for the campuses where the action takes place?

. . . . .

a. Fitzgerald, *This Side of Paradise*

b. Faulkner, *The Sound and the Fury*

c. Cather, *My Ántonia*

d. Wolfe, *Of Time and the River*

e. Joyce, *A Portrait of the Artist as a Young Man*

f. Ellison, *Invisible Man*

1. University College, Dublin

2. University of Nebraska

3. Tuskegee Institute

4. Washington Square College of New York University

5. Harvard University

6. Princeton University

Immortal
Autumn

———❧———

*P*oets tend to take autumn very seriously. Maybe this is because of their well-known vested interest in misery. Autumn is the season when Mother Nature begins packing it up for the year, and as the sap recedes, so does cosmic optimism. The best the poets can muster is a philosophical transcendence of the whole business: "I cry to you beyond upon this bitter air," as A. MacLeish once put it (the emphasis is on the "beyond"). The lines that follow are from well-known poems having to do with autumn. Can you match the letters of the quotations with the numbers of the authors? The titles of the poems from which the lines are taken are given with the answers. (Incidentally, the author of the fifth excerpt cited was mistaken; many an insect or plant has been hoodwinked by Indian summer into springlike activity.)

· · · · ·

a. And comes that other fall we name
    the fall
  He says the highway dust is over all

b. I come to pick your berries harsh
    and crude,
  And with forced fingers rude,
  Scatter your leaves before the
    mellowing year

c. That time of year thou mayst in me
    behold
  When yellow leaves or none, or few
    do hang

d. O what can ail thee, knight-at-arms,
  So haggard and so woebegone?
  The squirrel's grainery is full,
  And the harvest's done

e. Oh fraud that cannot cheat the
    Bee —
  Almost thy plausibility
  Induces my belief

f. Ah, Distinctly I remember,
  It was in the bleak December,
  And each separate dying ember
  Wrought its ghost upon the floor

g. Autumn days in our section
   Are the most used-up thing on earth
   (Or in the waters under the earth)

1. John Milton

2. Edgar Allan Poe

3. Emily Dickinson

4. William Shakespeare

5. Robert Frost

6. John Crowe Ransom

7. John Keats

Poetic
Trees

*O*nly God can make a tree, according to Joyce Kilmer anyway, but poets certainly know how to make use of them. Robert Frost considered it absolutely essential that poets remain in contact with trees at all times. Addressing his remarks to a "Window Tree" (not to be confused with a bay window), he declared that "my sash is lowered when night comes on / But let there never be curtain drawn / Between you and me." No poet has ever been known to complain about there being too many trees around; they like to leave that sort of thing to real estate developers and highway departments. On the other hand it is apparently legitimate to protest about not being able to see the forest for the trees, and William Morris even claimed that "the woods have no voice but the voice of complaining." Reader, have you ever heard a tree complain? Willows have been known to weep, aspens to quake and tremble, and ponderosas to pine, but no one has ever heard a word of complaint from a tree, not even from a sourwood or a bitter elm. (Dante did make a tree trunk shriek, come to think of it, but that was in Hell.) Can you name the poets and the poems in which the seven kinds of trees below have roles?

· · · · ·

a. birch

b. chestnut

c. live oak

d. tamarind

e. laurel

f. elm

g. pine

Death

———— ❧ ————

Writers remain intrigued by this subject — which is understandable, since there are no firsthand reports about what happens. We know about Macbeth's days lighting fools their way to dusty death, and Death be not proud, and Come delicate death serenely arriving, arriving, and Because I could not stop for death, and so on. But each of the following authors produced at least one work in which the word "death" appears in the title itself. Can you match the author with the title?

· · · · ·

a. Willa Cather

b. Eudora Welty

c. Robert Frost

d. Dylan Thomas

e. James Agee

f. Arthur Miller

g. Randall Jarrell

1. *A Death in the Family*

2. *Death of a Salesman*

3. "The Death of the Ball Turret Gunner"

4. "A Refusal to Mourn the Death by Fire of a Child in London"

5. "Death of a Traveling Salesman"

6. "The Death of the Hired Man"

7. *Death Comes for the Archbishop*

Something
In Common

———— ❧ ————

What do the following all have in common?

· · · · ·

a. a well-known book publisher who died in 1984

b. an English poet laureate

c. the addressee of a series of letters in a baseball novel

d. a ninth-century English king

e. the speaker of a dramatic monologue written by a twentieth-century poet

f. a popular brand of tobacco

g. the king of Belgium during World War I

h. the 1928 Democratic party presidential candidate

i. a Confederate general fatally wounded at the battle of Shiloh

Double
Duty

——— ❧ ———

*N*ow here's a tricky one. Each of the titles that follow has been used by at least two different authors, for works written in at least two different literary genres. Can you name both for each?

· · · · ·

a. Fire and Ice

b. Blackberry Winter

c. A Farewell to Arms

d. The Old Wives' Tale

e. Porphyria's Lover

f. The Dead

g. Shiloh

The Bard
Of Avon

*N*ext to the King James Bible, the works of William Shakespeare have furnished more book titles than any other work by any other author in the English language. People find it hard to believe that anyone without a college education could have written them, so there is a lengthy list of better-educated writers who have each been proposed as his ghostwriter. The best guess thus far is that they were written by another person with the same name. And what would a book of literary quizzes be without one on the Bard of Avon? So—each of the titles given below derives ultimately from a Shakespeare play. Can you match the title with the play?

· · · · ·

a. Somerset Maugham, *Cakes and Ale*

b. Noel Coward, *Pomp and Circumstance*

c. William Faulkner, *The Sound and the Fury*

d. John Steinbeck, *The Winter of Our Discontent*

e. Ogden Nash, "Very like a Whale"

f. Frederick Forsyth, *The Dogs of War*

g. Michael Yatron, *The Lunatic, the Lover, and the Poet*

1. *Twelfth Night*

2. *A Midsummer Night's Dream*

3. *Julius Caesar*

4. *Othello*

5. *Macbeth*

6. *Hamlet*

7. *Richard III*

Musical
Lines

❧

*O*ne of the worst poems in the English language, all things considered, is "The Symphony," by Sidney Lanier. In that late nineteenth-century effusion, the poet, who also played the flute, attempted to represent the various orchestral instruments in language. For example, the "melting clarionet" disposes as follows: "'O Trade! O trade!' the Lady Said, / 'I too wish thee utterly dead / If all thy heart is in thy head. / For O my God! and O my God.'" (Now does that sound even remotely like Benny Goodman?) Or the bassoons, "Like weird / Gray-beard / Old harpers sitting on the high sea-dunes, / Chanting runes." You get the idea. However, musical instruments do frequently appear in poems. Can you match the verses below with the poets? The titles of the poems from which the lines are taken are given with the answers.

· · · · ·

a. At the round earth's imagined
   corners, blow
   Your trumpets

b. A damsel with a dulcimer
   In a vision once I saw

c. The harp that once through Tara's
   halls

d. The double double double beat
   Of the thundering drum

e. Or hear old Triton blow his
   wreathèd horn

f. Tom-tom, c'est moi. The blue guitar
   And I are one

g. In perfect phalanx to the Dorian
   mood
   Of flutes and recorders

1. Thomas Moore

2. Wallace Stevens

3. John Donne

4. William Wordsworth

5. John Milton

6. Samuel Taylor Coleridge

7. John Dryden

Houses

————— ❧ —————

*I*n the House of Fiction, declared Henry James, there are many windows. To carry James's metaphor a little further, the view through some windows (say, Samuel Beckett's) is more opaque than others. Some are of stained glass (George Eliot), and some of magnifying glass (William Faulkner). Sometimes the windows are in need of washing (Erskine Caldwell, Henry Miller), and sometimes they show a crack or two (Herman Wouk, etc.) Some of the windows are made of clear plastic (Harold Robbins, say); others have frosted glass in them (Agatha Christie, etc.). Some windows are curtained (Jane Austen), and some are in dire need of curtains (Jack Kerouac). Occasionally the windows turn out to be mirrors (John Barth). And so on. But anyway, houses often figure in the titles of books and stories. Can you identify the author and title from each of the following descriptions?

· · · · ·

a. This New England house was renowned for the number of gables it contained.

b. This novel of the 1960s is about a painter who spends considerable time in France and Italy before settling down to work in Charleston, South Carolina.

c. A midwestern academic gentleman lived in this particular dwelling.

d. This nineteenth-century English novel helped reform the English courts of chancery.

e. This nineteenth-century French novel is set in an Italian duchy.

f. A visitor to this dwelling barely managed to get out before it disintegrated.

g. The heroine of this early twentieth-century novel by an Afro-American author is brought up in a home set up by her white father for his black mistress.

Noted Fictional Athletes

———❧———

*I*n addition to windows, the House of Fiction can also contain golf links, baseball diamonds, basketball and tennis courts, boxing rings, and other provisions for a sound mind in a sound body (one hopes). Can you match the fictional athlete with the sport that each plays? (There are two baseball players and two golfers in the lineup.) The authors and titles of the works in which the characters appear are given with the answers.

. . . . .

a. Rabbit Angstrom

b. Tom Stark

c. Milton Loftis

d. Jordan Baker

e. Robert Cohn

f. Roy Hobbs

g. Jack Keefe

1. boxing

2. football

3. golf

4. basketball

5. baseball

Admonitory
Words

———❦———

Walker Percy once compared the so-called apocalyptic novel to the canaries that miners used to carry into coal mines. If the canary passed out, it was a warning that something was wrong with the air. Other authors can be more direct about it. The lines of verse that follow are words of admonition; the poet is engaged in giving orders, warnings, and the like. Can you match the following admonitions with the poets who delivered them? The titles of the works in which they appear are given with the answers.

· · · · ·

a. Hence loathèd Melancholy

b. Be off, or I'll kick you downstairs!

c. Go, dumb-born book

d. Up, lad: when the journey's over
There'll be time enough to sleep

e. Not fare well,
But fare forward, voyagers

f. Be calm, thou Wedding-Guest

g. Take O take those lips away
That so sweetly were forsworn

1. Ezra Pound

2. T. S. Eliot

3. Samuel Taylor Coleridge

4. John Milton

5. William Shakespeare

6. Lewis Carroll

7. A. E. Housman

The Sea
Around Us

_S_amuel Johnson declared that life aboard a ship was like life in a prison, with the additional chance of being drowned. It depends on the viewpoint. Joseph Conrad rather liked it, as did Captain Marryat, Herman Melville, and William McFee. Mark Twain claimed that the happiest years of his life were spent as a pilot on the Mississippi, but strangely he never wrote about piloting, only about learning how to do it. James Fenimore Cooper practically invented the sea story. Lord Byron encouraged Shelley to take up sailing, with the result that poor Bysshe was drowned. William Faulkner once built a sailboat but didn't write about it. It isn't necessary to go to sea to write about it: Walt Whitman and Edna St. Vincent Millay got good poems merely out of riding on ferryboats. The following are some poetic effusions concerning the sea. Name the poet and the poem for each.

· · · · ·

a. I must go down to the sea again

b. The sea of faith was once, too, at the full

c. I should have been a pair of ragged claws
   Scuttling across the floors of silent seas

d. And may there be no moaning of the bar
   When I put out to sea

e. That dolphin-torn, that gong-infested sea

f. The sea whisper'd me

Musical
Motifs

*E*ach of the following real or imagined musical compositions plays a distinctive role in a literary work. Match the composition with the literary work.

· · · · ·

a. "Für Elise"

b. "Old Hundred" (the Doxology)

c. "Are You Washed in the Blood of the Lamb?"

d. the Vinteuil Sonata

e. "Lá Ci Darem La Mano"

f. "Just a Baby's Prayer at Twilight"

1. *Remembrance of Things Past* (Proust)

2. *Look Homeward, Angel* (Wolfe)

3. "General William Booth Enters into Heaven" (Lindsay)

4. "June Recital" (Welty)

5. *Ulysses* (Joyce)

6. *Adventures of Tom Sawyer* (Twain)

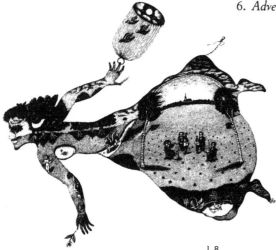

Important Addresses

———❦———

W hat famous literary characters would you be likely to run into at the following addresses?

· · · · ·

a. 221-B Baker Street, London

b. Elsinore Castle, Denmark

c. "Satis House," London

d. 7 Eccles Street, Dublin

e. "Dixieland," Altamont, North Carolina

f. "The Tabard," Southwark

g. Fitzgerald and Moy's saloon, Chicago

Railroad Anthems

*T*he day of the railroad as the principal mode of intercity travel may be done, but in its time trains inspired many a poet to rhapsodic utterance. Can you match these particular poetic references to trains with the authors? The names of the poems in which the lines appear are given with the answers.

· · · · ·

a. After the first powerful plain
  manifesto
  The black statement of pistons,
  without more fuss
  But gliding like a queen, she leaves
  the station

b. I like to see it lap the Miles —
  And lick the valleys up —
  And stop to feed itself at Tanks —
  And then — prodigious step

c. Type of the modern — emblem of
  motion and power — pulse of the
  continent,
  For once come serve the Muse and
  merge in verse, even as here I see
  thee

d. As a train that travels underground
  track
  Feels current flashed from far-off
  dynamos,
  Our wheels whirling with impetus
  elsewhere
  Generated we run, are ruled by rails

e. And Pullman breakfasters glide
  glistening steel
  From tunnel into field — iron strides
  the dew —
  Straddles the hill, a dance of wheel
  on wheel.
  You have a half-hour's wait at
  Siskiyou,
  Or stay the night and take the next
  train through

f. Sing in your gravel, in your clean
  gully.
  Let the moaning railroad trains go
  by.
  Till they stop you, go on with your
  song

1. Hart Crane

2. Carl Sandburg

3. Emily Dickinson

4. Stephen Spender

5. C. Day Lewis

6. Walt Whitman

Melancholy Days

*B*oredom is an all-too-frequent subject for poets. It isn't that they get more bored than other people, but that the subject seems to be especially amenable to poetry. Who are the following bored poets, and what are the names of the works?

. . . . .

a. To-morrow, and to-morrow, and to-
    morrow,
   Creeps in this petty pace from day to
    day

b.   The hot water at ten.
   And if it rains, a closed car at four,
   And we shall play a game of chess,
   Pressing lidless eyes and waiting for
    a knock upon the door

c. Man comes and tills the fields and
    lies beneath,
   And after many a summer dies the
    swan.
   Me only cruel immortality
   Consumes

d. I am sick o' wastin' leather on these
    gritty pavin'-stones,
   An' the blasted English drizzle
    wakes the fever in my bones;
   Though I walks with fifty

   'ousemaids outer Chelsea to the
    Strand,
   An' they talks a lot o' lovin', but wot
    do they understand?

e. And I was desolate and sick of an
    old passion,
    Yea, I was desolate and bowed my
     head:
   I have been faithful to thee, Cynara!
    in my fashion

f. Miniver cursed the commonplace
    And eyed a khaki suit with
     loathing;
   He missed the mediæval grace
    Of iron clothing

g. There's a certain slant of light,
   Winter afternoons —
   That oppresses, like the Heft
   Of Cathedral Tunes —

Winter
Remembered

Winter is icumen in, lhude singe goddamme. Put away the hammock, rake up the remaining leaves, have the antifreeze checked, bring the potted plants inside, install the storm windows, get out the red flannel underwear, turn up the thermostat, brew yourself a cup of Oolong, and see whether you can match the titles of these wintry-sounding works with the names of their authors.

. . . . .

a. "Silent Snow, Secret Snow"

b. "Snowbound"

c. "Fire and Ice"

d. "The Snow Man"

e. *Winterset*

f. "The Cross of Snow"

g. "Winter Remembered"

1. Henry Wadsworth Longfellow

2. John Greenleaf Whittier

3. John Crowe Ransom

4. Robert Frost

5. Maxwell Anderson

6. Conrad Aiken

7. Wallace Stevens

Gifts
Outright

——— ❦ ———

Not only is it better to give than to receive presents, but it can also make for very good fiction. Identify the author and the work in which each of the following situations involving gifts occurs.

· · · · ·

a. a music teacher gives her pupil a silver butterfly pin with a broken clasp

b. a husband gives his wife a set of combs

c. an employer gives an employee a prize turkey

d. a man buys his mistress a dog for their Manhattan apartment

e. a U. S. Army officer provides a bell for an Italian church

f. a wife gives her husband a Confederate major's coat

g. a youth gives his sister a phonograph record of the song, "Little Shirley Beans"

Truth
In Poetry

❧

Poets are, depending upon who is doing the defining, supposed to be concerned either with beauty, or truth, or both. Can you match the following well-known apostrophes to truth with the poets who penned the lines? The works in which the lines appear are given with the answers.

· · · · ·

a. Truth forever on the scaffold,
Wrong forever on the throne —
Yet that scaffold sways the future

b. I died for Beauty — but was Scarce
Adjusted in the Tomb
When one who died for Truth was
lain
In an adjoining room —

c. "Beauty is truth, truth beauty," that
is all
Ye know on earth, and all ye need to
know

d. We who seven years ago
Talked of honour and of truth
Shriek with pleasure if we show
The weasel's twist, the weasel's tooth

e. Truth, crushed to earth, shall rise
again;
The eternal years of God are here

f. He hath loosed the fateful lightning
of his terrible swift sword;
His truth goes marching on

g. One truth is clear, Whatever is, is
right

1. Julia Ward Howe

2. Alexander Pope

3. John Keats

4. James Russell Lowell

5. William Cullen Bryant

6. Emily Dickinson

7. William Butler Yeats

Delicious
Authors

❧

*W*orks of literature have been called nourishing, appetizing, tasty, delicious, savory, flavorful, and what have you. So let's think about food. How many writers can you think of whose names go with dining, drinking, etc.? Example: Joyce Carol Oates. We'll also accept close resemblances, if they're funny.

· · · · ·

What Trade
Art Thou?

———❧———

*S*cott Fitzgerald wrote that rich people were different; because they didn't have to work for a living, things that were ordinarily of secondary importance became inflated and took on major importance in their lives. To which his friend Hemingway responded, "Yes, they've got more money." Writers have found, even so, that people who are so unfortunate as to have to hold down jobs can make interesting characters in books. Can you identify the profession, trade, or occupation of each of the following characters and the author and literary work in which he/she appears?

· · · · ·

a. Lydgate

b. John Wellington Wells

c. Mr. Slope

d. Mr. Venus

e. Hetty Sorrel

f. Diggory Venn

g. Marlow

Family
Ties

———❧———

Remember those novels like Galsworthy's *The Forsyte Saga*, in which, to help the reader keep track of who was related to whom, the publisher included a foldout genealogical chart? Genealogy doesn't seem to be as much in vogue nowadays; perhaps the so-called "nuclear family" has done away with the preeminence of family relationships. If so, this will doubtless put a crimp in the style of writers of fiction. Each of the following authors wrote a work in which a family relationship is part of the title. Can you match the author with the title?

· · · · ·

a. Theodore Dreiser

b. Robert Penn Warren

c. Robert Graves

d. Clarence Day

e. D. H. Lawrence

f. Fyodor Dostoyevsky

g. Anton Chekhov

h. Patrick Dennis

1. *Life with Father*

2. *The Brothers Karamazov*

3. *Uncle Vanya*

4. *Sister Carrie*

5. *Auntie Mame*

6. *Sons and Lovers*

7. *Wife to Mr. Milton*

8. *Brother to Dragons*

Distinctive Families

*H*appy families may be all alike, but the families that follow manage to remain quite distinctive even as they have their ups and downs. Can you identify the author and the novel in which each of the following families is featured?

. . . . .

a. the Brangwens

b. the Buchans

c. the Micawbers

d. the Joads

e. the Addamses

f. the Bennets

Military History

*M*ilitary history—battles, campaigns, soldiers, sailors—frequently figures in works of poetry and fiction. See if you can match the military situation with the title of the work.

. . . . .

a. A seventeenth-century military captain debates whether to read about the wars of the Jews or Julius Caesar's campaigns in Gaul.

b. A retired English officer and corporal reenact the campaigns of the War of the Spanish Succession.

c. A political appointee receives a government job formerly held by a hero of the War of 1812.

d. A British sailor relives his life as he clings to a rock.

e. A miller's son listens with enthusiasm as a surgeon major recalls the Napoleonic campaigns.

f. A Confederate veteran writes magazine articles in New York City.

g. A Union veteran discusses war at a dinner in Boston.

1. *The Red and the Black* (Stendhal)

2. *The Rise of Silas Lapham* (Howells)

3. *The Scarlet Letter* (Hawthorne)

4. *The Courtship of Miles Standish* (Longfellow)

5. *Tristram Shandy* (Sterne)

6. *Pincher Martin* (Golding)

7. *The Bostonians* (James)

World War I

———— ❧ ————

The shock of the Great War of 1914–1918 upon the literary sensibility was profound, as Paul Fussell demonstrated so clearly in his book *The Great War and Modern Memory*. Not only that, but, paradoxically, even though the United States got in only at the tail end of the conflict and suffered far fewer battle casualties than any of the other major participants, the war's impact on American literature seemed most marked of all. Each of the following fictional characters—four Yanks and three Brits—was a participant in the war. Identify the author and the novel in which each appears.

· · · · ·

a. Frederic Henry

b. Christopher Tietjens

c. James Gatz

d. John Sartoris

e. Peter Wimsey

f. Denis Fairchild

g. Clifford Chatterley

Invocations
To the Muse

———— ❦ ————

*I*t used to be mandatory for a bard who was starting out to tell a lengthy tale to invoke the help of the appropriate muse. Although this posed no problems for the Greeks and Romans, later authors had considerable trouble with the requirement, so it was dropped. Still, it continues to be tried occasionally. We present here some well-known invocations. Can you match the invocation and the work?

· · · · ·

a. Muse, tell of the man of many
　　resources who wandered far and
　　wide after he sacked the holy city

b. Thou spirit, who led this glorious
　　Eremite
　　Into the desert, His victorious field,
　　Against the spiritual foe, and
　　brought'st Him thence
　　By proof the undoubted Son of God,
　　inspire,
　　As thou art wont, my prompted song

c. What dire offense from amorous
　　causes springs,
　　What mighty contests rise from
　　trivial things,
　　I sing—This verse to Caryll, Muse!
　　is due

d. American Muse, whose strong and
　　diverse heart

So many men have tried to
　　understand
But only made it smaller with their
　　art.
Because you are as various as your
　　land

e. Of Man's first disobedience, and the
　　fruit
　　Of that forbidden tree, whose mortal
　　taste
　　Brought death into the world and all
　　our woe,
　　With loss of Eden, till one greater
　　Man
　　Restore us and regain the blissful
　　seat,
　　Sing, Heav'nly Muse

f. Sing, O Goddess, the ruinous wrath
　　of Achilles,

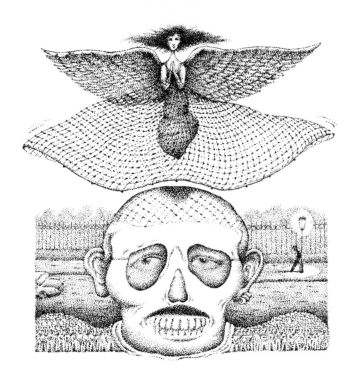

Son of Peleus, the terrible curse that
 brought
Unnumbered woes upon the
 Achaeans and hurled
To Hades so many heroic souls

g. Against all mortal critics bear me
 out in it, thou just Spirit of
 Equality, which hast spread one
 royal mantle of humanity over all
 my kind! Bear me out in it, thou
 great democratic God!

1. *Iliad* (Homer)

2. *Paradise Lost* (Milton)

3. *John Brown's Body* (Benét)

4. *Moby-Dick* (Melville)

5. *The Rape of the Lock* (Pope)

6. *Paradise Regained* (Milton)

7. *Odyssey* (Homer)

Real
Persons

R eal people, of the flesh-and-blood historical variety, wander into poems, stories, plays, and the like, and sometimes odd things happen to them there. The result is that many do not care to be made use of for such purposes. "I am not a character in a novel!" declared the librarian Richard Best when the BBC sought to interview him on the subject of James Joyce, in whose *Ulysses* Best figures; "I am a living being!" That was some years back; today he is only a character in a book. What follows is a series of lines from poems, each of which refers to a historical person. Who is the person, who is the poet, and what is the name of the poem?

· · · · ·

a. He disappeared in the dead of
   winter

b. And we left him alone with his glory

c. Others abide our question. Thou art
   free

d. He star'd at the Pacific

e. The Assyrian came down like a wolf
   on the fold

f. "Shoot if you must this old gray
      head,
   But spare your country's flag," she
      said

g. O Captain! my Captain! our fearful
   trip is done

Subtitles
Of Books

—❧—

*T*he vogue for giving subtitles to books has long since receded. Few readers tend to remember such things. Can you match the letters of the subtitles with the numbers of the titles of these literary works?

· · · · ·

a. *The Mistakes of a Night*

b. *Life Among the Lowly*

c. *A Novel without a Hero*

d. *A Study of Provincial Life*

e. *The History of a Foundling*

f. *'Tis Sixty Years Since*

g. *Virtue Rewarded*

1. *She Stoops to Conquer* (Goldsmith)

2. *Tom Jones* (Fielding)

3. *Waverley* (Scott)

4. *Uncle Tom's Cabin* (Stowe)

5. *Middlemarch* (Eliot)

6. *Pamela* (Richardson)

7. *Vanity Fair* (Thackeray)

Ship
Ahoy!

—❧—

A boat, the saying goes, is a hole in the water into which money is poured. A ship is a large boat, of the seagoing sort. Any definition attempting to explain the distinction between the two terms more specifically than that won't work. The vessels involved in the lines of poetry that follow are, or were, all ships rather than boats. None of the authors who wrote the lines were sailors, which is probably just as well, because all but one of the ships was in deep trouble, while the one that wasn't in trouble (in the last quotation) was engaged in founding a section of the country that for the next two hundred years or so caused a great deal of trouble for everybody else. See if you can match the lines with the ships. The author and the poem in which each ship appears is given with the answers.

· · · · ·

a. We have not struck, he composedly
   cried, We have just begun our
   part of the fighting

b. And the skipper had taken his little
   daughter to bear him company

c. And give her to the god of storms,
   the lightning and the gale!

d. Till the Spinner of the Years
   Said "Now!" And each one hears,
   And consummation comes, and jars
   two hemispheres

e. Dame, at our door
   Drowned, and among our shoals,
   Remember us in the roads, the
       heaven-haven of the Reward

f. The breaking waves dashed high
   On the stern and rock-bound coast,
   And the woods against a stormy sky
   Their giant branches tossed

1. *Mayflower*   4. *Deutschland*

2. *Constitution* 5. *Bonhomme Richard*

3. *Hesperus*   6. *Titanic*

Literary
Presidents

———— ❧ ————

W̶e have it on good authority that when President Richard M. Nixon was shown a set of the collected writings of Thomas Jefferson, he was astounded. And Alfred Kazin tells of the undergraduate college student who, upon being introduced to the speeches of Abraham Lincoln, was much impressed; who, he asked, was Lincoln's speechwriter? Of course American presidents nowadays simply don't have the time to write their own speeches, state papers, and so on. In some cases this is probably for the better; but other presidents have been quite skilled with the pen or the typewriter. Not many people realize, for example, that before World War II broke out, Dwight D. Eisenhower was several times given U.S. Army assignments because of his skill at writing. The titles that follow are of books written by, not for, U.S. presidents. Can you name the presidents?

· · · · ·

a. *The Winning of the West*

b. *At Ease*

c. *Constitutional Government in the United States*

d. *Notes on the State of Virginia*

e. *Poems of Religions and Society*

f. *Why England Slept*

g. *Discourses on Davila*

Tribulations
Of Teenagers

———❧———

*O*ne of the many frauds perpetrated upon the youth of America is the notion that their teens constitute the best years of their lives. This is nonsense, as every teenager knows; it is a falsehood perpetuated by aging adults who have forgotten the awkwardness, embarrassments, confusions, and frustrations of the young; they can remember the freckles but not the acne. Good novelists, however, know better. Can you match each of the following descriptions with the young'un and the short story or novel in which his or her tribulations are chronicled?

· · · · ·

a. Her father's a watch repairman, her mother is dead, her older brother is in the army and getting married, and she spends the better part of a summer sitting around the house with a little boy and a housekeeper.

b. Nobody in town thinks much of him, his younger brother is always trying to get him in trouble, and his girlfriend gets furious with him when he catches her sneaking a look at a forbidden book.

c. The family stories about her aunt's elopement are terribly romantic, but when she meets the man her aunt eloped with she is disillusioned, and another aunt's version of the story disillusions her still more.

d. He can't seem to enroll in school without getting sent home, and when his girlfriend has a date with a fellow student he doesn't trust, he goes berserk and gets into a fight, after which he checks into a hotel.

e. Her music teacher thinks she is sure to become a great concert pianist, but she takes a job playing the piano in a movie theater and eventually she ceases playing at all.

f. When his parents die, he goes to live with an uncle, who arranges to have him taken off to sea on a boat.

g. He and his sister are left in the care of an uncle, who hires a parson's daughter to look after them at a country estate.

1. Tom Sawyer — *Adventures of Tom Sawyer* (Twain)

2. Virgie Rainey — "June Recital" (Welty)

3. Frankie Addams — *The Member of the Wedding* (McCullers)

4. Miles — *The Turn of the Screw* (James)

5. David Balfour — *Kidnapped* (Stevenson)

6. Holden Caulfield — *The Catcher in the Rye* (Salinger)

7. Miranda — "Old Mortality" (Porter)

Relatives

———❧———

*A*ll things are relative, said Einstein. Relatives, of all things! said my Aunt Ruth. See if you can name the relative, the author, and the work.

. . . . .

a. Ursula Brangwen's sister

b. Mme Merle's daughter

c. Strephon's mother

d. Hippolytus' stepmother

e. Creon's son

f. Catherine Earnshaw's husband

g. Laertes's father

Ever-Returning
Spring

———— ❧ ————

*I*t is a Well Known Fact that poets are supposed to get into high gear in the spring-time. Can you match each of these apostrophes to the vernal equinox with the poet? The works containing the lines are given with the answers.

. . . . .

a. For I'm to be queen o' the May,
  mother, I'm to be Queen o' the
  May

b. O thou to whom the musical white
  spring
  Offers her lily undistinguishable

c. Whan the Aprill with his shoures
  soote
  The droghte of march has perced to
  the roote

d. Ever-returning spring, trinity sure to
  me you bring

e. By the rude bridge that arched the
  flood,
  Their flag to April's breeze unfurled

f. Spring, with that nameless pathos in
  the air
  Which dwells in all things fair

g. Laurel is green for a season, and love
  is sweet for a day;
  But love grows bitter with treason
  and laurel outlives not May

1. Alfred, Lord Tennyson

2. Ralph Waldo Emerson

3. Geoffrey Chaucer

4. E. E. Cummings

5. Algernon Charles Swinburne

6. Walt Whitman

7. Henry Timrod

When Homer Nodded

❧

*E*ven Homer nodded, as the saying goes; but, judging from the following examples of perfectly terrible verse, some of our most famous poets fell plumb asleep at the desk. Match each excerpt with the illustrious author. The works containing the lines are given with the answers.

. . . . .

a. On a smallpox victim:
   Each little pimple had a tear in it,
   To wail the fault its rising did
      commit

b. On a woman discovering her lover's
      corpse:
   At last they felt the kernal of
      the grave,
   And Isabella did not stamp
      and rave

c. A poet hoping for quiet outside his
      wedding chamber:
   Nor let th'unpleasant choir of
      frogs still croaking
   Make us to wish their choking

d. The eyes of the weeping Mary
      Magdalen:
   Two walking baths, two weeping
      motions,

Portable and compendious
   oceans

e. On a donkey:
   Once more the Ass, with motion
      dull,
   Upon the pivot of his skull
   Turned round his long left ear

f. A St. Bernard dog a bit after the
      nick of time:
   A traveller, by the faithful hound,
   Half-buried in the snow was
      found,
   Still grasping in his hands of ice
   That banner with the strange
      device,
      Excelsior!

42

1. Richard Crashaw

2. John Keats

3. William Wordsworth

4. Henry Wadsworth Longfellow

5. John Dryden

6. Edmund Spenser

Oh, to Be
In England

O h to be in England, / Now that Winston's out," Ezra Pound wrote in 1946 or so. (Ezra had wit, all right; but any poet who could prefer Benito Mussolini to Winston Churchill was either quite mad or else a mighty sorry excuse for a human being. We prefer to think the former.) Politically the British Empire isn't what it used to be; of that there's no question. But if you take England's record and put it next to that of any other empire, from Ancient Rome onward, it looks pretty good (except maybe as regards Ireland), and the poets who have celebrated it had reasonably good cause to do so. Here are quotations about England by five Britons plus one American and one Irishman. Can you name the authors and the works?

. . . . .

a. the further off from England, the
   nearer 'tis to France

b. Oh to be in England, now that
   April's here

c. Dirty British coaster with a salt-
   cased smoke-stack

d. I know the kings of England, and I
   quote the fights historical

e. That there's some corner of a
   foreign field
   That is forever England

f. a moment in the British camp, a
   moment and away

g. For England may keep faith
   For all that is done and said

Damsels
In Place

❦

*T*he spirit of place used to be thought of as a dryad. Literary places and literary females still go together. Match the places with the damsels they are associated with. The names of the poets and the titles of the works are given with the answers.

· · · · ·

a. South Clark Street

b. the Springs of Dove

c. Bath

d. the River Afton

e. Pike

f. somewhere east of Suez

g. Frederick Town

1. Supi-yaw-lat

2. unnamed, but presumably Lucy

3. Frankie

4. Barbara Frietchie

5. Betsy

6. Mary

7. Alison

Domestic
Difficulties

——— ❧ ———

Thy are known to all, though to some of us more than others. How dull life would be without some domestic fireworks. Can you match the following fictional situations with the literary works in which they take place?

. . . . .

a. A man whose wife has been unfaithful to him joins a Masonic lodge.

b. A woman rearranges the furniture, and her husband, returning home late at night, cracks his head against a sideboard.

c. A daughter comes upon her father in the arms of another woman at a country club.

d. A man takes a friend to see his mistress act in a play, and his friend falls in love with her.

e. A woman becomes angry when her nephew and her daughter travel to Chicago together.

f. A man finds that a supposedly valuable gift left to him by his uncle is worthless.

g. A woman changes her plans to be remarried when her fiancé takes her son's side in a family dispute.

1. *The Moviegoer* (Percy)

2. "The Bear" (Faulkner)

3. *The Ambassadors* (James)

4. *Ulysses* (Joyce)

5. *Sister Carrie* (Dreiser)

6. *War and Peace* (Tolstoy)

7. *Lie Down in Darkness* (Styron)

Literary Locales

---❧---

I think the sense of place is as essential to good and honest writing as a logical mind," wrote Eudora Welty; "surely they are somewhere related. It is by knowing where you stand that you grow able to judge where you are." An odd thing about the literary imagination is that the more deeply grounded it is in the particularities of a specific place—deeply grounded, that is, not just decked out with surface details—the more universal it is apt to be in its appeal. Can you name the poets and the poems in which the following places figure?

. . . . .

a. Tilbury Town

b. Sir John's Hill

c. the Gort Forge

d. Eton College

e. Deering's Woods

f. Kermanshah

g. Walsingham

Take Me out
To the Ball Game

———— ❧ ————

The last names of the following members of the Major League Baseball Hall of Fame are also the last names of well-known British or American authors. Here are the ballplayers. Can you name their literary equivalents?

. . . . .

a. Ty Cobb

b. Eddie Collins

c. Candy Cummings

d. Whitey Ford

e. Bucky Harris

f. Walter Johnson

g. Sam Rice

h. Jackie Robinson

i. Ted Williams

j. George Wright

Concerning
Bees

—❦—

*H*ow are you on works about bees? Match the following lines about bees with the titles of the works from which they are taken.

· · · · ·

a. And I laugh to see them whirl and
   flee,
   Like a swarm of golden bees,
   While I widen the rent in my wind-
   built tent

b. Where the bee sucks, there suck I,
   In the cowslip's bell I lie

c. The moan of doves in immemorial
   elms,
   And murmuring of innumerable
   bees

d. Nine bean-rows will I have there, a
   hive for the honey-bee,
   And live alone in the bee-loud glade

e. It was a transmogrifying bee
   Came droning down on Chucky's old
   bald head
   And sat and put the poison

f. Hide me from day's garish eye,
   While the bee with honied thigh

That at her flowery work doth sing

g. And the song she was singing ever
   since
   In my ear sounds on: —
   "Stay at home, pretty bees, fly not
   hence!
   Mistress Mary is dead and gone!"

1. *The Princess* (Tennyson)

2. "L'Allegro" (Milton)

3. "The Cloud" (Shelley)

4. *The Tempest* (Shakespeare)

5. "Janet Waking" (Ransom)

6. "Telling the Bees" (Whittier)

7. "The Lake Isle of Innisfree"
   (Yeats)

Colorful Writing

*I*t was a great day for European culture when you learned to swear in yellow," Stephen Dedalus tells his friend Lynch in James Joyce's *A Portrait of the Artist as a Young Man.* And, in a somewhat different rhetorical mode, Sir Philip Sidney wrote that "nature never set forth the earth in so rich tapestry, as divers poets have done, neither with pleasant rivers, fruitful trees, sweet smelling flowers; nor whatsoever else may make the too much loved earth more lovely." Each of the following descriptions is of a work whose title contains a reference to one of the colors of the spectrum. Color yourself purple if you fail to match more than two descriptions with their titles.

· · · · ·

a. a novel by William Henry Hudson about an elusive young girl in the jungles of Venezuela

b. a late-Victorian quarterly whose art editor was Aubrey Beardsley

c. a novel by the French author Stendhal about a crime of passion

d. a Civil War novel by Stephen Crane

e. an account by William Least Heat Moon about a journey across America in search of the author's Native American identity

f. a hound dog's tale by Frederick Benjamin Gipson, recently revived as a movie

1. *Blue Highways*

2. *Old Yeller*

3. *Green Mansions*

4. *The Red Badge of Courage*

5. *The Yellow Book*

6. *The Red and the Black*

Literature Into Music

———❧———

Y ou can nearly always get a good argument going among musical theorists if you bring up the matter of program music: a musical composition, that is, which supposedly describes a particular event, or object, or real-life subject. Can it, in fact, be done? (If you heard Rimsky-Korsakov's "The Flight of the Bumble Bee" and didn't already know it had to do with a bee, would you be able to guess it? Is the Beethoven Symphony No. 6, the Pastorale, successful because it has a specific program, or in spite of it, or does the program have any relevance to it one way or the other?) This is a problem in aesthetics: can an abstract art form such as music be translated into the concrete particularities of literature, or vice versa? Whichever way you decide, it is undeniable that composers do frequently resort to literature as subjects for musical compositions. Each of the following literary works has been made into a musical composition. Can you name both the author and the composer?

a. *Egmont*

b. "Ode for St. Cecilia's Day"

c. *Faust*

d. "The Lorelei"

e. *Carmen*

f. *Thus Spake Zarathustra*

g. *The Marriage of Figaro*

Battles and Campaigns

———— ❧ ————

*E*ach of the following battles or military campaigns plays a part in a well-known literary work. Match each fracas with the work that involves it.

· · · · ·

a. Waterloo

b. the bombardment of Fort McHenry

c. the sea fight between the *Serapis* and the *Bonhomme Richard*

d. Borodino

e. the siege of Namur

f. Caporetto

g. Agincourt

1. "Song of Myself" (Whitman)

2. *War and Peace* (Tolstoy)

3. *Childe Harold's Pilgrimage* (Byron)

4. *Henry V* (Shakespeare)

5. "The Star-Spangled Banner" (Key)

6. *A Farewell to Arms* (Hemingway)

7. *Tristram Shandy* (Sterne)

Literary
Clergymen

❦

*T*his is a two-part question. (1) How many of the following literary clergymen and clergywomen, ordained or self-appointed, can you identify? Name the author and the work in which each appears.

. . . . .

a. Father Conmee, S.J.

b. the Rev. Gail Hightower

c. Elmer Gantry

d. Pastor Manders

e. Parson Adams

f. the Rev. Theobald Pontifex

g. Daddy Faith

h. Sister Bessie

i. Parson Yorick

(2) How many works of fiction can you name in which a sermon is delivered and the text of the sermon becomes part of the fiction?

FORTY SEVEN.

Poems
About Flowers

*H*ere are descriptive lines about flowers from six poems. Can you match the descriptions with the posies being described? The poets and poems are given with the answers.

. . . . .

a. The purple petals, fallen in the pool,
   Made the black water with their
      beauty gay

b. Wee, modest, crimson-tippèd flow'r,
   Thou's met me in an evil hour

c. Ah_____! weary of time,
   Who countest the steps of the sun

d. Branches they bore of that
      enchanted stem,
   Laden with flower and fruit, whereof
      they gave
   To each

e.   thy term is reached,
   Thy leaf hangs loose and bleached;
   Bees pass it by unimpeached

f. Thou blossom bright with autumn
      dew,
   And colored with the earth's own
      blue

1. sunflower

2. rhodora

3. lotus

4. gentian

5. daisy

6. rose

Marriages

❧

*I*n romances, marriages come at the end; in novels, at the beginning. Can you identify the authors and the works of fiction in which the following marriages are involved?

. . . . .

a. Irene and Soames Forsyte

b. Christina and Theobald Pontifex

c. George and Emily Gibbs

d. Eliza and Oliver Gant

e. H. C. Earwicker and Anna Livia Plurabelle

f. Carol and Will Kennicott

g. Isabel and Gilbert Osmond

Opening
Lines

—·❋·—

Certain works of fiction are so well known that their opening lines can be readily identified. Can you match the following opening lines with the works they open?

· · · · ·

a. In the late summer of that year we lived in a house in a village that looked across the river and the plain to the mountains.

b. Miss Brook had that kind of beauty which seems to be thrown into relief by poor dress.

c. Once upon a time and a very good time it was there was a moocow coming down along the road and this moocow that was coming down along the road met a nicens little boy named baby tuckoo.

d. The nickname of the train was the Yellow Dog. Its real name was the Yazoo-Delta.

e. The small town of Verrières may be regarded as one of the most attractive in the Franche-Comté.

f. One fine day in early summer a young man lay thinking in Central Park.

g. Whether I shall turn out to be the hero of my own life, or whether that station will be held by anyone else, these pages must show.

h. If I am out of my mind, it's all right with me, thought Moses H_____ .

i. I wish either my father or my mother, or indeed both of them, as they were in duty both equally bound to it, had minded what they were about when they begot me.

j. Well, prince, so Genoa and Lucca are now just family estates of the Buonapartes.

k. At a certain village in *La Mancha*, which I shall not name, there liv'd not long ago one of those old-fashion'd Gentlemen who are never without a Lance upon a Rack, an old Target, a lean Horse, and a Greyhound.

l. For a long time I used to go to bed early.

m. Sitting beside the road, watching the wagon mount the hill toward her, Lena thinks, "I have come from Alabama: a fur piece. All the way from Alabama, a-walking. A fur piece."

n. On an exceptionally hot day in July a young man came out of the garret in which he lodged in S. Place and walked slowly, as though in hesitation, towards K. bridge.

o. "Tom!"
No answer.
"Tom!"
No answer.

p. If you really want to hear about it, the first thing you'll probably want to know is where I was born, and what my lousy childhood was like, and how my parents were occupied and all before they had me, and all that David Copperfield kind of crap, but I don't feel like going into it, if you want to know the truth.

1. *Remembrance of Things Past* (Proust)

2. *The Last Gentleman* (Percy)

3. *The Catcher in the Rye* (Salinger)

4. *Middlemarch* (Eliot)

5. *Light in August* (Faulkner)

6. *A Portrait of the Artist as a Young Man* (Joyce)

7. *Herzog* (Bellow)

8. *Adventures of Tom Sawyer* (Twain)

9. *David Copperfield* (Dickens)

10. *A Farewell to Arms* (Hemingway)

11. *Don Quixote* (Cervantes)

12. *Crime and Punishment* (Dostoyevsky)

13. *Tristram Shandy* (Sterne)

14. *The Red and the Black* (Stendhal)

15. *Delta Wedding* (Welty)

16. *War and Peace* (Tolstoy)

Sibling Rivalry

❧

*S*ibling rivalries have been going on ever since Adam and Eve had difficulties with their two boys. Writers of fiction, as might be expected, have made much use of the doings of brothers and sisters. Can you match the following groups of siblings with the appropriate family names? The authors and the titles of the novels in which the families appear are given with the answers.

· · · · ·

a. Jo, Amy, Beth, Meg

b. Dmitri, Alyosha, Ivan

c. Scarlett, Suellen, Carreen

d. Ann, Jolyon, James, Swithin, Roger, Julia, Hester, Nicholas, Timothy, Susan

e. Thomas, Sidney, Mary

f. Nicholas, Peter, Vera, Natasha

g. Daisy, Steve, Helen, Luke, Ben, Grover, Eugene

1. Forsyte

2. Gant

3. Karamazov

4. Rostov

5. March

6. O'Hara

7. Sawyer

Titles
Needed

~ ❧ ~

Y ou can't judge a book by its cover, or sometimes even by its title. The question that follows is kind of tricky, like an English crossword puzzle as compared to the American variety. What you are asked to do is to supply titles of literary works in accordance with hypothetical situations. For example, "a Communist medal for bravery under fire" could be *The Red Badge of Courage*; "what good children have on Christmas eve" could be *Great Expectations*; "attempting to kindle a cigar with a butane lighter on a sailboat" might be *The Light That Failed*. Now see what you can do with these.

· · · · ·

a. a novel by Aldous Huxley selected by a quail hunter

b. a novel by Thomas Wolfe and a play by Eugene O'Neill selected by a ticket agent at the bus station

c. a poem by John Milton checked out by a crapshooter seeking to repair his fortunes

d. a poem by Wallace Stevens selected by a dieting gourmet

e. a Cormac McCarthy novel bought by a hematologist

f. an animal husbandry student's selection from E. E. Cummings

Literary Vessels

❧

Novels, poems, narratives of the sea have been popular at least since Jonah's troubles with the whale. Here are the names of seven ships of various sizes and types. Name the author and the literary work in which each appears.

. . . . .

a. *Grampus*

b. SS *Patna*

c. USS *Caine*

d. SS *Quaker City*

e. HMS *Somerset*

f. whaling ship *Pequod*

g. SS *Glencairn*

Places in
Literary History

❦

*T*he following are all names of places that have figured in American and English literary history. Identify each.

. . . . .

a. Porlock

b. Missolonghi

c. Pamplona

d. Cock Lane

e. the Temple of Jupiter in Rome

f. the Chicago stockyards

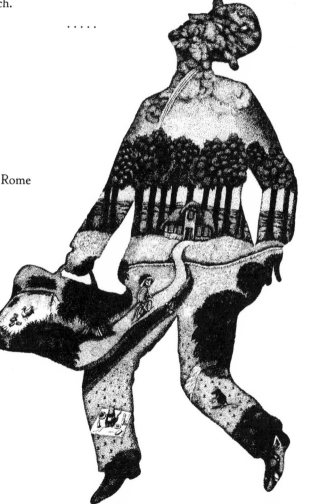

Tending To Virginia

——— ❧ ———

*T*he Commonwealth of Virginia has been the locale or subject of numerous books. Here are the titles of a few. Can you match them with their authors?

. . . . .

a. *The Virginian*

b. *Virginia Is a State of Mind*

c. *In Ole Virginia*

d. *The Vanishing Virginian*

e. *Virginia*

f. *The Virginians*

1. William Makepeace Thackeray

2. Virginia Moore

3. Owen Wister

4. Rebecca Yancey Williams

5. Ellen Glasgow

6. Thomas Nelson Page

Pen Names

———— ✿ ————

Some authors use pen names so regularly that their actual names are known but to few. Others publish under both their pen names and their real names. Can you match the following pseudonyms with the real names of the authors?

· · · · ·

a. a novelist who signed herself George Eliot

b. a French novelist and close friend of the composer Chopin who wrote under the name of George Sand

c. an urbane and cynical writer of short stories who called himself Saki

d. an imagist poet who used only her initials, H. D.

e. a twentieth-century British novelist and essayist who published under the name of George Orwell

f. a British military adventurer and Arabist who used the name T. E. Shaw for several of his publications

g. a poet and theorist of the Irish Literary Renaissance known as A. E.

1. Eric Blair

2. T. E. Lawrence

3. Amandine Aurore Dupin

4. George W. Russell

5. Hilda Doolittle

6. Mary Ann Evans

7. Hector H. Munro

More
Flowers

——— ❧ ———

*S*ay it with flowers," the song goes. Or as Leopold Bloom thinks in *Ulysses*, "Language of flowers. They like it because no-one can hear. . . . Angry tulips with you darling manflower punish your cactus if you don't please forgetmenot how I long violets to dear roses when we soon anemone meet all haughty nightstalk wife Martha's perfume." And the Bard himself: "There's rosemary, that's for remembrance. And there is pansies, that's for thought." Reader, did you know that Scarlett O'Hara was originally named Pansy? Whether you did or you didn't, see if you can fill in the botanicals in the following lines, and identify the authors and works.

a. Oh _____, thou are sick!

b. In a _____ bell I lie

c. The _____ weaves her fringes

d. Yet once more, oh ye _____ and once more

e. There once was a Dormouse who lived in a bed
   Of _____ (blue) and _____ (red)

f. breeding _____ out of the dead land

g. A host of golden _____

Saints of New England

Whatever its other sins may have been, New England has long been known as the birthplace and home of famous authors. Very well, the following is a list of fifteen writers whose work is identified in one way or the other with New England. Of them, four were actually not born there. Which four? Their birthplaces are also given with the answers.

· · · · ·

a. Louisa May Alcott

b. Emily Dickinson

c. Ralph Waldo Emerson

d. Robert Frost

e. Nathaniel Hawthorne

f. Oliver Wendell Holmes

g. Sarah Orne Jewett

h. Henry Wadsworth Longfellow

i. James Russell Lowell

j. Robert Lowell

k. J. P. Marquand

l. Edwin Arlington Robinson

m. Wallace Stevens

n. Henry David Thoreau

o. John Greenleaf Whittier

Parodies

The art of literary parody has a long and often unsavory history. Some writers—Wordsworth, Whitman—seem at times almost to parody themselves. What follows are some lines that capture the peculiarities of a writer's idiom well enough that you ought to be able to match the parodies with the authors being parodied. The names of the parodists are given with the answers.

· · · · ·

a. Gin a body meet a body
   Flyin' through the air,
   Gin a body hit a body,
   Will it fly? and where?

b. Behind a cloud his mystic sense,
   Deep hidden, who can spy?
   Bright as the night when not a star
   Is shining in the sky

c. A classic waits for me, it contains all,
   nothing is lacking,
   Yet all were lacking if taste were
   lacking, if the endorsement of the
   right man were lacking

d. I dwelt in Delta Epsilon—
   A fairer house—than yours—
   No footprints—on the
   windowsills—
   No mirrors—on the doors—

e. As we get older we do not get any
   younger

f. I saw the best minds of my
   generation
   Destroyed—Marvin
   Who spat out poems; Potrzebie
   Who coagulated a new bop
   literature in fifteen
   Novels

g. Here's a mellow cup of tea, golden
   tea!
   What a world of rapturous thought
   its fragrance brings to me!
   Oh, from out the silver cells
   How it wells!
   How it smells, smells, smells!

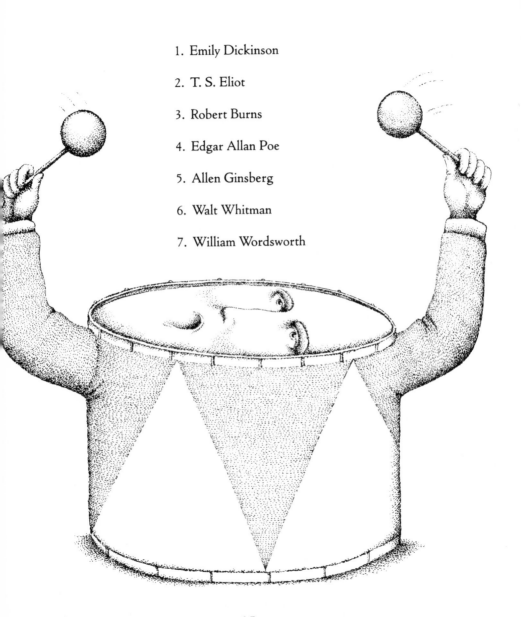

1. Emily Dickinson

2. T. S. Eliot

3. Robert Burns

4. Edgar Allan Poe

5. Allen Ginsberg

6. Walt Whitman

7. William Wordsworth

Summertime

———✤———

Summertime, and the living is easy. . . ." And so is this particular quiz, which is appropriate, for who would want voluntarily to cause trouble in the summer? Henry James thought that the most beautiful words in the English language were "summer afternoon." For those who must labor physically in the summer, to be sure, it can be otherwise. "Heat-brutal August," Thomas Wolfe wrote in remembering his job at Langley Field, Virginia, in the summer of 1918. And General Grant proposed to fight it out on the line of the Wilderness "if it takes all summer"—which indeed it did, and the succeeding fall and winter as well. In any event, try matching the following titles with the authors (two are by the same author).

· · · · ·

a. *Summer and Smoke*

b. *The Boys of Summer*

c. *New England: Indian Summer*

d. *After Many a Summer Dies the Swan*

e. *A Midsummer Night's Dream*

f. *Suddenly Last Summer*

1. Aldous Huxley

2. Tennessee Williams

3. William Shakespeare

4. Roger Kahn

5. Van Wyck Brooks

Succinct Definitions

The ability to define something succinctly or wittily is no mean feat. Can you identify the authors of the following definitions?

· · · · ·

a. A cow is of the bovine ilk;
   One end is moo, the other milk

b. Puritanism — The haunting fear that
   someone, somewhere, may be
   happy

c. Hope is the thing with feathers —

d. As I would not be a slave, so I would
   not be a master. This expresses
   my idea of democracy

e. LEXICOGRAPHER: a maker of
   dictionaries; a harmless drudge

f. A foolish consistency is the
   hobgoblin of little minds

g. Fame is the spur that the clear spirit
   doth raise
   (That last infirmity of noble mind)

For
The Birds

———— ❦ ————

Some birds make for good poetry; others just do not. It seems unfair. When William Cullen Bryant wrote "To a Waterfowl," he was careful not to name the particular kind of bird he had in mind; was it a duck? a goose? Walt Whitman described the gander as crying "Ya-honk!" It was not one of his more successful lines; with the spotted hawk he did rather better. Wordsworth wrote poems about linnets, Coleridge about an albatross, Shelley a skylark, Keats an owl (Wordsworth did, too, only his was stuffed). Sidney Lanier essayed the marsh-hen—"as the marsh-hen secretly builds on the watery sod / Behold I will build me a nest on the greatness of God"; alas, not even being rhymed with the Almighty could make a marsh-hen poetic. Browning wrote of crop-filled crows, Tennyson of bats. Then there was Poe's raven: "Much I marveled this ungainly fowl to hear discourse so plainly / Though its answer little meaning—little relevancy bore." At that, it is better than the parrot that he said was the first bird that came to mind when he was writing that poem. Did a poet write about a cowbird or a blue-faced booby? Has anyone written good poems about the duckcissel, the purple gallinule, or the pelican (whose beak can hold more than his bellican)? What of the yellow-bellied sapsucker, tufted titmouse, pigeon, widgeon, and turkey? The ptarmigan, the limpkin, the stork? Poets, to your goose quills! Meanwhile, name the ornithological authors of these lines about our feathered friends and the poems the lines appear in.

· · · · ·

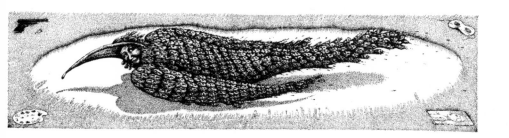

a. The redbreast whistles from a
    garden croft,
  And gathering swallows twitter in
    the skies

b. The only moving thing
  Was the eye of the blackbird

c. Over Sir John's hill,
  The hawk on fire hangs still

d. Upon the brimming water among
    the stones
  Are nine and fifty swans

e. O Cuckoo! shall I call thee Bird,
  Or but a wandering Voice!

f. To hear an oriole sing
  May be a common thing

g. There is a singer everyone has
    heard,
  Loud, a mid-summer and a mid-
    wood bird

What's
In a Name?

❧

*H*ere is a group of writers, all of whom share the same given name: Henry. Let's see how well you can spot the identity of each from a fact or two about their lives. Match the descriptions with the authors' names.

. . . . .

a. This man's widely popular autobiography was first published for general readers several years after his death.

b. This American poet was a college classmate of Nathaniel Hawthorne at Bowdoin.

c. This poet was born into a Jewish family, converted to Christianity, and died in Paris.

d. This playwright shocked playgoers of the day by writing a play dealing with the hereditary effects of syphilis.

e. This novelist suffered a mysterious injury while helping to extinguish a fire.

f. This English writer made a highly controversial decision to leave the Anglican church and become a Roman Catholic.

g. This writer's occupation was the manufacture of lead pencils.

1. Henry James

2. Heinrich Heine

3. Henry David Thoreau

4. John Henry Newman

5. Henry Adams

6. Henrik Ibsen

7. Henry Wadsworth Longfellow

Paying Jobs

——— ❧ ———

Art may be its own reward, but writers have to eat, too. The following questions concern ways in which some of them paid their bills.

· · · · ·

a. William Faulkner's appearance on a U.S. postal stamp reminded many people that he once worked as postmaster of University, Mississippi. Name a prolific British novelist who also worked at the P.O.

b. What English poet served as Latin secretary to Oliver Cromwell?

c. Edmund Spenser wrote *The Faerie Queene* while holding a series of posts in Queen Elizabeth's government. In what country did he serve?

d. What great American writer served for nineteen years as a customs official in New York City?

e. What eighteenth-century novelist was a magistrate?

f. Name at least three authors, from three different centuries, who were trained as physicians.

Liquid
Lines

———— ❧ ————

*I*dentify the following liquid lines. Match the excerpt with the title of the poem.

· · · · ·

a. I hear lake water lapping

b. The stationary blasts of waterfalls

c. The unplumb'd, salt, estranging sea

d. I do not know much about gods; but
    I think that the river
    Is a strong brown god

e.   building high
    Over the chained bay waters Liberty

f. How wanton thy waters her snowy
    feet lave

g. The maker's rage to order words of
    the sea

1. "To Marguerite, Continued"
   (Arnold)

2. "Afton Water" (Burns)

3. *The Prelude VI* (Wordsworth)

4. "The Idea of Order at Key West"
   (Stevens)

5. "To Brooklyn Bridge" (Crane)

6. "The Lake Isle of Innisfree"
   (Yeats)

7. "The Dry Salvages" (Eliot)

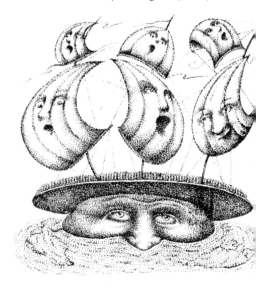

Compote

*T*he titles of the works cited below combine in a literary compote of rare and delicate flavor. Can you identify the author of each aromatic ingredient?

· · · · ·

a. "After Apple-Picking"

b. *A Clockwork Orange*

c. *The Cherry Orchard*

d. "Nine Nectarines and Other Porcelain"

e. *The Grapes of Wrath*

f. *Strange Fruit*

g. *The Kandy-Kolored Tangerine-Flake Streamline Baby*

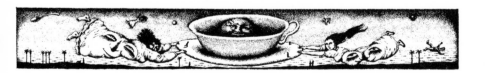

The Gentle Art of Name-Dropping

*N*ame-dropping — the mentioning of a famous or highly regarded name as if in passing, to suggest that one has a close relationship with same — is one of the oldest forms of human activity, dating at least back to 2 Kings 9:20: "The driving is like the driving of Jehu, the son of Nimshi; for he driveth furiously." Probably the most assiduous name-dropper in the history of the belles lettres was James Boswell, who made a literary career out of knowing Samuel Johnson, but others such as William Dean Howells (*My Mark Twain*), Edward John Trelawney (*Recollections of the Last Days of Shelley and Byron*), and Aaron Hotchner (*Papa Hemingway*) were pretty good at it, too. Your major-league name-dropper never appears to be mentioning an acquaintance with the great or near-great just for the sake of pride — "shake the hand that shook the hand of John L. Sullivan." He does it en passant, as if corroborating a point in casual conversation — "that's exactly what Hank Kissinger was saying last week." Skilled name-droppers use nicknames and diminutives whenever possible — "Bill Faulkner," "Poppy Bush," "Tom Eliot," "Ollie North," and so on. Poets are usually very good at name-dropping. In each of the following excerpts, the poet addresses one of his predecessors in the craft. Match the name-droppings with the poems containing them.

· · · · ·

a. My Shakespeare, rise: I will not
      lodge thee by
   Chaucer, or Spenser, or bid
      Beaumont lie
   A little further, to make thee a room

b. Ah Ben [Jonson]!
   Say how, or when
   Shall we thy guests
   Meet at those lyric feasts

c. Milton! Thou should'st be living at
      this hour

d. You, Andrew Marvell

e. I make a pact with you, Walt
      Whitman —
   I have detested you long enough

f. Where are we going, Walt
      Whitman? The doors close in an
      hour.
   Which way does your beard point
      tonight?

1. "A Supermarket in California"
   (Ginsberg)

2. "You, Andrew Marvell"
   (MacLeish)

3. "To the Memory of My
   Beloved . . . Shakespeare"
   (Jonson)

4. "A Pact" (Ezra Pound)

5. "An Ode for Him" (Herrick)

6. "London, 1802" (Wordsworth)

Foul Weather

❦

—————

Whⁿen in doubt, discuss the weather" is a good rule to follow in making conversation. Everybody will have an opinion on the subject. Can you give the authors and titles of the works in which these famous bad-weather descriptions occur?

. . . . .

a. Blow, winds, and crack your cheeks:
    Rage, blow!
    You cataracts and hurricanoes, spout
    Till you have drench'd our steeples

b. After a while I went out and left the
    hospital and walked back to the
    hotel in the rain.

c. All in a hot and copper sky,
    The bloody sun, at noon,
    Right up above the mast did stand,
    No bigger than the moon

d. Yes, the newspapers were right;
    snow was general all over Ireland.

e. The night is freezing fast,
    To-morrow comes December;
    And winterfalls of old
    Are with me from the past;
    And chiefly I remember
    How Dick would hate the cold

f. Just the worst time of the year
    For a journey, and such a long
    journey;
    The ways deep and the weather
    sharp,
    The very dead of winter

g. The brooks were frozen, the air-
    ports almost deserted,
    And snow disfigured the public
    statues;
    The mercury sank in the mouth of
    the dying day

Famous
Dates

❧

We all hated learning them in school, but dates can be important, especially the literary ones. They anchor what we know. How can we be sure that the Battle of Hastings came before the discovery of America, if it weren't for our having been made to memorize 1066 and 1492? We needn't, like the Major-General in *The Pirates of Penzance*, be able to name all the kings of England or "quote the fights historical / From Marathon to Waterloo in order categorical," but to know when certain important events took place is a Good Thing. Try these on for size.

. . . . .

a. Name two great Elizabethan playwrights born in 1564.

b. In what year were Eliot's *Adam Bede*, Mill's *On Liberty*, and Darwin's *The Origin of Species* all published?

c. In what year were Faulkner's *The Sound and the Fury*, Wolfe's *Look Homeward, Angel*, and Hemingway's *A Farewell to Arms* all published?

d. What great modern novel is set on June 16, 1904?

e. Who, in Shakespeare's play as in life, met his comeuppance on the Ides of March?

f. What, according to T. S. Eliot, is the cruellest month, and where does he say so?

g. Who wrote both "Dry September" and *Light in August*?

Parodies
And Parodied

———❧———

"The style is the man," a Frenchman, probably the Comte de Buffon, once remarked. Writers do have their own way of putting things. Each of the items that follows is a rendering, in the style of one writer, of certain well-known poetic lines or fictional passages of another writer. If you can identify both the particular styles being parodied, and the original versions of the lines that are being paraphrased, you're pretty good. (P.S.—One of the styles used is not that of a particular author, but of a certain kind of writing.)

· · · · ·

a. Ah, but that's just the selfish point of it all, don't you see? That in proposing my own so very personal monstrance I implicate *you*. I don't apologize, I don't so much as ask leave of you for so presuming. I see of course what you mean—one's ever so chary of offending. It's only that one does go on, you know, and if one's not always precisely the thing one hopes to be, still there's the sharing. Oh dear yes, the ever so common uniqueness—call it that. So we *do* reach out, I'm afraid. Isn't that just what makes it bearable? For both parties, I make bold. That we're alone, and yet not. That *is* the oddity.

b. Pursuant to regulation 1023–234–AC, as modified by directive NJ–203 dated 3 Oct 14, it is suggested recipient arrive 1 Beacon St Boston MA, ETA 1900 hrs EST, to accompany undersigned on inspection downtown city. It is also suggested recipient wear clothing appropriate for conditions of moderate humidity incl likelihood fog.

c. To build a barrier—of Stone—
Is direst Patronage—
Nor all the folk—of Nature's realm
Respect such Persiflage

But turn — in Carefree Comedy —
To setting it Awry —
As if to say — Exclusion
Be Contrareity

d. The assembled elders, attired in locomotive-gray togs that would have made a mortician plead for levity, sported whiskers tonsured after the manner of the Smith Bros. Atop the collected crania was a set of headware commissioned by Sir Christopher Wren to publicize the construction of the steeple on St. Paul's Cathedral. Such females as were present elected to enliven the proceedings with variegated hoods in assorted sere and dun, with the exception of a corporal's guard who showed up sans millinery of any kind whatever. As is meet on all such official occasions, the citizenry lined up at the front door of the *calaboza*, a dainty portal of four-inch-thick oak ornamented with track spikes and designed to discourage widows, panhandlers and members of the working press from seeking entry.

e. "As to the degree of arborescence, you are to remember that the proper office of the poet is neither to manufacture that which was never seen, nor to contest with nature for what is appropriate to nature only. He who would number the varieties of foliage or reproduce the intricacies of ramiformity must soon concede the greater veracity of the natural object itself." B————. "But, sir, do you make no allowance for the poet's genius in this respect?" J————. "Sir, I make all the allowance proper to the matter, which is none whatsoever. (smiling) I do not say, mind you, that there is not in *Scotland* an ample field for the exercise of genius in imagining trees! Ha ha!"

1. *Urban Bards*: **a-4** William Wordsworth, "Composed upon Westminster Bridge"; **b-2** Carl Sandburg, "Chicago"; **c-5** Walt Whitman, "Crossing Brooklyn Ferry"; **d-4** William Blake, "London"; **e-3** Samuel Taylor Coleridge, "Cologne"; **f-6** William Butler Yeats, "Easter 1916"; **g-1** Robert Lowell, "For the Union Dead"

2. *The Strenuous Life*: **a.** Henry David Thoreau, *A Week on the Concord and Merrimack Rivers*; **b.** Ernest Hemingway, *The Sun Also Rises*; **c.** Mark Twain, *Adventures of Tom Sawyer*; **d.** James Boswell, *The Journal of a Tour to the Hebrides with Dr. Samuel Johnson*: **e.** Marcel Proust, *Remembrance of Things Past*; **f.** Geoffrey Chaucer, *The Canterbury Tales*; **g.** Henry Adams, *The Education of Henry Adams*

3. *Bright College Years*: **a-6; b-5; c-2; d-4; e-1; f-3**

4. *Immortal Autumn*: **a-5** "The Oven Bird"; **b-1** "Lycidas"; **c-4** Sonnet LXXIII; **d-7** "La Belle Dame Sans Merci"; **e-3** "These are the days when birds come back"; **f-2** "The Raven"; **g-6** "Conrad in Twilight"

5. *Poetic Trees*: **a.** Robert Frost, "Birches," or Henry Wadsworth Longfellow, "Song of Hiawatha"; **b.** Henry Wadsworth Longfellow, "The Village Blacksmith," or William Butler Yeats, "Among School Children"; **c.** Walt Whitman, "I Saw in Louisiana a Live-Oak Growing," or Sidney Lanier, "Marshes of Glynn"; **d.** Edgar Allan Poe, "To Science"; **e.** John Milton, "Lycidas"; **f.** Alfred, Lord Tennyson, *The Princess*; **g.** Henry Wadsworth Longfellow, "Evangeline," or Jean Toomer, "Georgia Dusk." (If you thought of others, they will do equally well.)

6. *Death*: **a-7; b-5; c-6; d-4; e-1; f-2; g-3**

7. *Something in Common*: They're all known as Al for short: **a.** Alfred A. Knopf; **b.** Alfred, Lord Tennyson; **c.** in *You Know Me, Al* (Ring Lardner); **d.** Alfred the Great; **e.** "The Love Song of J. Alfred Prufrock" (T. S. Eliot); **f.** Prince Albert; **g.** Albert I; **h.** Alfred E. Smith; **i.** Albert Sidney Johnston

8. *Double Duty*: **a.** Robert Frost (poem) and Wallace Stegner (novel); **b.** John Crowe Ransom (poem) and Robert Penn Warren (short story); **c.** George Peele (poem) and Ernest Hemingway (novel); **d.** George Peele (drama) and Arnold Bennett (novel); **e.** Robert Browning (poem) and Ferrol Sams (novel); **f.** Rupert Brooke (poem) and James Joyce (novella);

g. Herman Melville (poem) and Shelby Foote (novel)

9. *The Bard of Avon*: **a-1; b-4; c-5; d-7; e-6; f-3; g-2**

10. *Musical Lines*: **a -3** "At the Round Earth's Imagined Four Corners"; **b-6** "Kubla Khan"; **c-1** "The Harp That Once through Tara's Halls"; **d-7** "Ode for St. Cecilia's Day, 1687"; **e-4** "The World Is Too Much with Us"; **f-2** "The Man with the Blue Guitar"; **g-5** Paradise Lost

11. *Houses*: **a.** Nathaniel Hawthorne, *The House of the Seven Gables*; **b.** William Styron, *Set This House on Fire*; **c.** Willa Cather, *The Professor's House*; **d.** Charles Dickens, *Bleak House*; **e.** Stendhal, *The Charterhouse of Parma*; **f.** Edgar Allan Poe, "The Fall of the House of Usher"; **g.** Charles Chesnutt, *House Behind the Cedars*

12. *Noted Fictional Athletes*: **a-4** John Updike, *Rabbit, Run*; **b-2** Robert Penn Warren, *All the King's Men*; **c-3** William Styron, *Lie Down in Darkness*; **d-3** F. Scott Fitzgerald, *The Great Gatsby*; **e-1** Ernest Hemingway, *The Sun Also Rises*; **f-5** Bernard Malamud, *The Natural*; **g-5** Ring Lardner, *You Know Me, Al*

13. *Admonitory Words*: **a-4** "L'Allegro"; **b-6** "Father William"; **c-1** "L'Envoi: Hugh Selwyn Mauberley"; **d-7** "Reveille"; **e-2** "The Dry Salvages"; **f-3** "Rime of

the Ancient Mariner"; **g-5** *Measure for Measure*

14. *The Sea around Us*: **a.** John Masefield, "Sea Fever"; **b.** Matthew Arnold, "Dover Beach"; **c.** T. S. Eliot, "The Love Song of J. Alfred Prufrock"; **d.** Alfred, Lord Tennyson, "Crossing the Bar"; **e.** William Butler Yeats, "Byzantium"; **f.** Walt Whitman, "Out of the Cradle Endlessly Rocking"

15. *Musical Motifs*: **a-4 ; b-6; c-3; d-1; e-5; f-2**

16. *Important Addresses*: **a.** Sherlock Holmes of the many stories by Sir Arthur Conan Doyle; **b.** Hamlet of Shakespeare's play; **c.** Miss Havisham and Estella of Charles Dickens's *Great Expectations*; **d.** Leopold and Molly Bloom of James Joyce's novel *Ulysses*; **e.** Eliza Gant and family of Thomas Wolfe's *Look Homeward, Angel*; **f.** host Harry Bailly and other pilgrims of Geoffrey Chaucer's *The Canterbury Tales*; **g.** George Hurstwood of Theodore Dreiser's *Sister Carrie*

17. *Railroad Anthems*: **a-4** "The Express"; **b-3** "I like to see it lap the Miles"; **c-6** "To a Locomotive in Winter"; **d-5** "As One Who Wanders into Old Workings"; **e-1** *The Bridge*; **f-2** "On a Railroad Right of Way"

18. *Melancholy Days*: **a.** William Shakespeare, *Macbeth*; **b.** T. S. Eliot, "The

Waste Land"; **c.** Alfred, Lord Tennyson, "Tithonus"; **d.** Rudyard Kipling, "The Road to Mandalay"; **e.** Ernest Dowson, "Cynara" ("Non Sum Qualis Eram Bonæ Sub Regno Cynaræ"); **f.** Edwin Arlington Robinson, "Miniver Cheevy"; **g.** Emily Dickinson, "There's a certain slant of light"

19. *Winter Remembered*: **a-6; b-2; c-4; d-7; e-5; f-1; g-3**

20. *Gifts Outright*: **a.** Eudora Welty, "June Recital"; **b.** O. Henry, "The Gift of the Magi"; **c.** Charles Dickens, *A Christmas Carol*; **d.** F. Scott Fitzgerald, *The Great Gatsby*; **e.** John Hersey, *A Bell for Adano*; **f.** Margaret Mitchell, *Gone with the Wind*; **g.** J. D. Salinger, *The Catcher in the Rye*

21. *Truth in Poetry*: **a-4** "The Present Crisis"; **b-6** "I died for Beauty"; **c-3** "Ode on a Grecian Urn"; **d-7** "Nineteen Hundred and Nineteen"; **e-5** "The Battlefield"; **f-1** "Battle Hymn of the Republic"; **g-2** "Essay on Man"

22. *Delicious Authors*: For starters, try these: Max Apple, Francis Bacon, Max Beerbohm, Wendell Berry, Albert J. Beveridge, Morris Bishop, René de Chateaubriand, Kelly Cherry, Charles Chesnutt, John Esten Cooke, George Crabbe, Stephen Duck, Stanley Fish, H. W. Fowler, Mother Goose (ha!), Philip Hamburger, Bret Harte, James Hogg, Thomas Kyd, Charles Lamb, Margaret Mead, Eric Partridge, Howard Pease, Katherine Anne Porter, Peter Quennell, Elmer Rice, E. P. Roe, Saki (H. H. Munro), Thomas Shadwell, Gertrude Stein, Rex Stout, Sir John Suckling, George Woodcock. (As for near misses, how about A. R. Almonds, Stephen Vincent Benne, Philip Broth, Richard Chaser, Maurice Cointreau, F. Marion Crawfish, Remy de Gourmand, Graham Greens, Rider Haddock, John Hollandaise, John Lox [ouch!], Alfred de Mussel, Dorothy Parkerhouse, Ezra Poundcake, Felix Saltine, Lincoln Stuffins, Allen Tater, Hans Waffle, William Butler Yeast?)

23. *What Trade Art Thou?*: **a.** doctor — George Eliot, *Middlemarch*; **b.** magician — W. S. Gilbert, *The Sorcerer*; **c.** cleric — Anthony Trollope, *Barchester Towers*; **d.** taxidermist — Charles Dickens, *Our Mutual Friend*; **e.** dairymaid — George Eliot, *Adam Bede*; **f.** reddleman — Thomas Hardy, *The Return of the Native*; **g.** seaman — Joseph Conrad, *Heart of Darkness* or *Lord Jim*

24. *Family Ties*: **a-4; b-8; c-7; d-1; e-6; f-2; g-3; h-5**

25. *Distinctive Families*: **a.** D. H. Lawrence, *Women in Love* and *The Rainbow*; **b.** Allen Tate, *The Fathers*; **c.** Charles Dickens, *David Copperfield*; **d.** John Steinbeck, *The Grapes of Wrath*; **e.** Carson McCullers, *The Member of the Wedding*;

f. Jane Austen, *Pride and Prejudice*

26. *Military History*: **a-4**; **b-5**; **c-3**; **d-6**; **e-1**; **f-7**; **g-2**

27. *World War I*: **a.** Ernest Hemingway, *A Farewell to Arms*; **b.** Ford Madox Ford, *Parade's End*; **c.** F. Scott Fitzgerald, *The Great Gatsby*; **d.** William Faulkner, *Sartoris (Flags in the Dust)*; **e.** Dorothy Sayers, any of the Lord Peter Wimsey novels; **f.** Eudora Welty, *Delta Wedding*; **g.** D. H. Lawrence, *Lady Chatterley's Lover*

28. *Invocations to the Muse*: **a-7**; **b-6**; **c-5**; **d-3**; **e-2**; **f-1**; **g-4**

29. *Real Persons*: **a.** William Butler Yeats — W. H. Auden, "In Memory of W. B. Yeats"; **b.** Sir John Moore — Charles Wolfe, "The Burial of Sir John Moore at Corunna"; **c.** William Shakespeare — Matthew Arnold, "Shakespeare"; **d.** Hernando Cortés — John Keats, "On First Looking into Chapman's Homer" (Keats confused Cortés with Balboa); **e.** Sennacherib — Lord Byron, "The Destruction of Sennacherib"; **f.** Stonewall Jackson — John Greenleaf Whittier, "Barbara Frietchie"; **g.** Abraham Lincoln — Walt Whitman, "O Captain! My Captain!"

30. *Subtitles of Books*: **a-1**; **b-4**; **c-7**; **d-5**; **e-2**; **f-3**; **g-6**

31. *Ship Ahoy!*: **a-5** Walt Whitman, "Song of Myself"; **b-3** Henry Wadsworth Longfellow, "The Wreck of the Hesperus"; **c-2** Oliver Wendell Holmes, "Old Ironsides"; **d-6** Thomas Hardy, "Convergence of the Twain"; **e-4** Gerard Manley Hopkins, "The Wreck of the Deutschland"; **f-1** Felicia Hemans, "The Landing of the Pilgrim Fathers in New England"

32. *Literary Presidents*: **a.** Theodore Roosevelt; **b.** Dwight D. Eisenhower; **c.** Woodrow Wilson; **d.** Thomas Jefferson; **e.** John Quincy Adams; **f.** John F. Kennedy; **g.** John Adams

33. *Tribulations of Teenagers*: **a-3**; **b-1**; **c-7**; **d-6**; **e-2**; **f-5**; **g-4**

34. *Relatives*: **a.** Gudrun — D. H. Lawrence, *Women in Love*; **b.** Pansy — Henry James, *The Portrait of a Lady*; **c.** Iolanthe — W. S. Gilbert, *Iolanthe*; **d.** Phaedra — Euripides, *Hippolytus*, or Racine, *Phèdre*; **e.** Haemon — Sophocles, *Antigone*; **f.** Edgar Linton — Emily Brontë, *Wuthering Heights*; **g.** Polonius — William Shakespeare, *Hamlet*

35. *Ever-Returning Spring*: **a-1** "The May Queen"; **b-4** "O Thou to Whom the Musical White Spring"; **c-3** *The Canterbury Tales*; **d-6** "When Lilacs Last in the Dooryard Bloom'd"; **e-2** "Concord Hymn"; **f-7** "Spring"; **g-5** "Hymn to Proserpine"

36. *When Homer Nodded*: **a-5** "On the Death of the Lord Hastings"; **b-2** "Isabella; or, the Poet of Basil"; **c-6** "Epithalamion"; **d-1** "The Weeper"; **e-3** "Peter Bell"; **f-4** "Excelsior"

37. *Oh, to Be in England*: **a.** Lewis Carroll, *Alice's Adventures in Wonderland*; **b.** Robert Browning, "Home Thoughts, from Abroad"; **c.** John Masefield, "Cargoes"; **d.** W. S. Gilbert, "The Major General's Song," *Iolanthe*; **e.** Rupert Brooke, "The Soldier"; **f.** William Cullen Bryant, "The Song of Marion's Men"; **g.** William Butler Yeats, "Easter 1916"

38. *Damsels in Place*: **a-3** anonymous song, "Frankie and Johnnie"; **b-2** William Wordsworth, "She Dwelt Among the Untrodden Ways"; **c-7** Geoffrey Chaucer, "The Miller's Tale," *The Canterbury Tales*; **d-6** Robert Burns, "Afton Water"; **e-5** anonymous song, "Sweet Betsy from Pike"; **f-1** Rudyard Kipling, "The Road to Mandalay"; **g-4** John Greenleaf Whittier, "Barbara Frietchie"

39. *Domestic Difficulties*: **a-6; b-4; c-7; d-5; e-1; f-2; g-3**

40. *Literary Locales*: **a.** Edwin Arlington Robinson, "Mr. Flood's Party"; **b.** Dylan Thomas, "Over Sir John's Hill"; **c.** William Butler Yeats, "To Be Carved upon a Stone at Thor Ballylee"; **d.** Thomas Gray, "Ode on a Distant Prospect of Eton College"; **e.** Henry Wadsworth Longfellow, "My Lost Youth"; **f.** Archibald MacLeish, "You, Andrew Marvell"; **g.** Robert Lowell, "The Quaker Graveyard at Nantucket," or Sir Walter Ralegh, "Walsenghame"

41. *Take Me out to the Ball Game*: **a.** Irvin S. or Humphrey Cobb; **b.** William or Wilkie Collins; **c.** E. E. Cummings; **d.** John, Ford Madox, or Richard Ford; **e.** Joel Chandler or Frank Harris; **f.** Samuel or James Weldon Johnson; **g.** Elmer, Cale Young, or Alice Hegan Rice; **h.** Edwin Arlington Robinson; **i.** William Carlos, Jonathan, Ben Ames, or Tennessee Williams; **j.** James or Richard Wright

42. *Concerning Bees*: **a-3; b-4; c-1; d-7; e-5; f-2; g-6**

43. *Colorful Writing*: **a-3; b-5; c-6; d-4; e-1; f-2**

44. *Literature into Music*: **a.** Goethe/Beethoven; **b.** Dryden/Handel; **c.** Goethe/Gounod; **d.** Heine/Schubert; **e.** Mérimée/Bizet; **f.** Nietzsche/Richard Strauss; **g.** Beaumarchais/Mozart

45. *Battles and Campaigns*: **a-3; b-5; c-1; d-2; e-7; f-6; g-4**

46. *Literary Clergymen*: **1. a.** James Joyce, *A Portrait of the Artist as a Young Man* and *Ulysses*; **b.** William Faulkner, *Light in August*; **c.** Sinclair Lewis, *Elmer Gantry*;

d. Henrik Ibsen, *Ghosts*; **e.** Henry Fielding, *Joseph Andrews*; **f.** Samuel Butler, *The Way of All Flesh*; **g.** William Styron, *Lie Down in Darkness*; **h.** Erskine Caldwell, *Tobacco Road*; **i.** Laurence Sterne, *Tristram Shandy*
2. For starters, *A Portrait of the Artist as a Young Man*, *Lie Down in Darkness*, and *Tristram Shandy*, above; also Herman Melville, *Moby-Dick*; and William Faulkner, *The Sound and the Fury*. Can you name any others?

47. *Poems about Flowers*: **a -2** Ralph Waldo Emerson, "The Rhodora"; **b-5** Robert Burns, "To a Mountain Daisy"; **c-1** William Blake, "Ah sunflower!"; **d-3** Alfred, Lord Tennyson, "The Lotos-Eaters"; **e-6** Robert Browning, "Women and Roses"; **f-4** William Cullen Bryant, "To the Fringed Gentian"

48. *Marriages*: **a.** John Galsworthy, *The Forsyte Saga*; **b.** Samuel Butler, *The Way of All Flesh*; **c.** Thornton Wilder, *Our Town*; **d.** Thomas Wolfe, *Look Homeward, Angel*; **e.** James Joyce, *Finnegans Wake*; **f.** Sinclair Lewis, *Main Street*; **g.** Henry James, *The Portrait of a Lady*

49. *Opening Lines*: **a-10; b-4; c-6; d-15; e-14; f-2; g-9; h-7; i-13; j-16; k-11; l-1; m-5; n-12; o-8; p-3**

50. *Sibling Rivalry*: **a-5** Louisa May Alcott, *Little Women*; **b-3** Fyodor

Dostoyevsky, *The Brothers Karamazov*; **c-6** Margaret Mitchell, *Gone with the Wind*; **d-1** John Galsworthy, *The Forsyte Saga*; **e-7** Mark Twain, *Adventures of Tom Sawyer*; **f-4** Leo Tolstoy, *War and Peace*; **g-2** Thomas Wolfe, *Look Homeward, Angel*

51. *Titles Needed*: **a.** *Point Counter Point*; **b.** *You Can't Go Home Again* and *Long Day's Journey into Night*; **c.** *Paradise Regained*; **d.** "No possum, no sop, no taters"; **e.** *Blood Meridian*; **f.** "The way to hump a cow"

52. *Literary Vessels*: **a.** Edgar Allan Poe, "Narrative of Arthur Gordon Pym"; **b.** Joseph Conrad, *Lord Jim*; **c.** Herman Wouk, *The Caine Mutiny*; **d.** Mark Twain, *Innocents Abroad*; **e.** Henry Wadsworth Longfellow, "The Midnight Ride of Paul Revere"; **f.** Herman Melville, *Moby-Dick*; **g.** Eugene O'Neill, SS *Glencairn* plays

53. *Places in Literary History*: **a.** English town where the "person" came from who supposedly interrupted Samuel Taylor Coleridge while he was composing "Kubla Khan"; **b.** place in Greece where Lord Byron died; **c.** Spanish city where the bullfights take place in Ernest Hemingway's *The Sun Also Rises*; **d.** street in London where Dr. Samuel Johnson investigated the ghost; **e.** ruins where Edward Gibbon heard the friars singing and determined to write *The Decline and Fall of the Roman Empire* (in actuality the ruins were those of the temple of Juno);

f. the locale of Upton Sinclair's *The Jungle*

54. *Tending to Virginia*: **a-3; b-2; c-6; d-4; e-5; f-1**

55. *Pen Names*: **a-6; b-3; c-7; d-5; e-1; f-2; g-4**

56. *More Flowers*: **a.** rose — William Blake, "The Sick Rose"; **b.** cowslip — William Shakespeare, *The Tempest*; **c.** gentian — Emily Dickinson, "The gentian weaves her fringes"; **d.** laurels — John Milton, "Lycidas"; **e.** delphiniums, geraniums — A. A. Milne, "The Dormouse and the Doctor"; **f.** lilacs — T. S. Eliot, "The Waste Land"; **g.** daffodils — William Wordsworth, "Daffodils"

57. *Saints of New England*: **a.** Alcott — Germantown, Pennsylvania; **d.** Frost — San Francisco, California; **k.** Marquand — Wilmington, Delaware; **m.** Stevens — Reading, Pennsylvania

58. *Parodies*: **a-3** James Clerk-Maxwell; **b-7** Hartley Coleridge; **c-6** E. B. White; **d-1** William Harmon; **e-2** Henry Reed; **f-5** Louis Simpson; **g-4** Barry Pain

59. *Summertime*: **a-2; b-4; c-5; d-1; e-3; f-2**

60. *Succinct Definitions*: **a.** Ogden Nash; **b.** H. L. Mencken; **c.** Emily Dickinson; **d.** Abraham Lincoln; **e.** Samuel Johnson;

f. Ralph Waldo Emerson; **g.** John Milton

61. *For the Birds*: **a.** John Keats, "Ode to Autumn"; **b.** Wallace Stevens, "Thirteen Ways of Looking at a Blackbird"; **c.** Dylan Thomas, "Over Sir John's Hill"; **d.** William Butler Yeats, "The Wild Swans at Coole"; **e.** William Wordsworth, "To a Cuckoo"; **f.** Emily Dickinson, "To hear an oriole sing"; **g.** Robert Frost, "The Oven Bird"

62. *What's in a Name?*: **a-5; b-7; c-2; d-6; e-1; f-4; g-3**

63. *Paying Jobs*: **a.** Anthony Trollope; **b.** John Milton; **c.** Ireland; **d.** Herman Melville; **e.** Henry Fielding; **f.** among others, François Rabelais (sixteenth century); Sir Thomas Browne (seventeenth century); Oliver Goldsmith, John Arbuthnot, and Tobias Smollett (eighteenth century); Walker Percy, William Carlos Williams, Merrill Moore, and Ferrol Sams (twentieth century)

64. *Liquid Lines*: **a-6; b-3; c-1; d-7; e-5; f-2; g-4**

65. *Compote*: **a.** Robert Frost; **b.** Anthony Burgess; **c.** Anton Chekhov; **d.** Marianne Moore; **e.** John Steinbeck; **f.** Lillian Smith; **g.** Tom Wolfe

66. *The Gentle Art of Name-Dropping*: **a-3; b-5; c-6; d-2; e-4; f-1**

67. *Foul Weather*: **a.** Shakespeare, *King Lear*; **b.** Ernest Hemingway, *A Farewell to Arms*; **c.** Samuel Taylor Coleridge, "Rime of the Ancient Mariner"; **d.** James Joyce, "The Dead"; **e.** A. E. Housman, "The Night Is Freezing Fast"; **f.** T. S. Eliot, "Journey of the Magi"; **g.** W. H. Auden, "In Memory of W. B. Yeats"

68. *Famous Dates*: **a.** William Shakespeare and Christopher Marlowe; **b.** 1859; **c.** 1929; **d.** James Joyce, *Ulysses*; **e.** Julius Caesar; **f.** April, in "The Waste Land"; **g.** William Faulkner

69. *Parodies and Parodied*: **a.** Walt Whitman, "Song of Myself": "I celebrate myself, and sing myself, / And what I assume you shall assume, / For every atom of me as good belongs to you";

b-5 Armed Services jargon — T. S. Eliot, "The Love Song of J. Alfred Prufrock": "Let us go then, you and I, / When the evening is spread out against the sky"; **c-1** Robert Frost, "Mending Wall": "Something there is that doesn't love a wall"; **d.** H.L. Mencken — Nathaniel Hawthorne, *The Scarlet Letter*, opening of Chapter 1: "A throng of bearded men, in sad-colored garments and gray, steeple-crowned hats, intermixed with women, some wearing hoods, and others bare-headed, was assembled in front of a wooden edifice, the door of which was heavily timbered with oak and studded with iron spikes"; **e.** James Boswell, *The Life of Samuel Johnson* — Joyce Kilmer, "Trees": "I think that I shall never see / A poem as lovely as a tree"